PIANO • VOCAL • GUITAR

SKYLAR GREY DON'T LOOK DOWN

ISBN 978-1-4803-5507-1

HAL•LEONARD®
CORPORATION

7777 W. BLUEMOUND RD. P.O. BOX 13819 MILWAUKEE, WI 53213

Visit Hal Leonard Online at
www.halleonard.com

BACK FROM THE DEAD

Words and Music by SKYLAR GREY,
Sean Anderson, ROSS GOLAN,
JONATHAN ROTEM and TRAVIS BARKER

Moderately fast

I nev-er thought _ that

you and I __ would ev-er meet __ a- gain. __ I

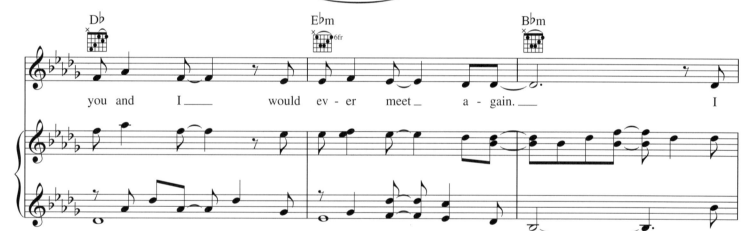

mourn the loss __ of you __ some- times, _ and pray for peace _ with- in. __

The word "dis - traught" can not des - cribe

how my heart has been, but where do we be - gin

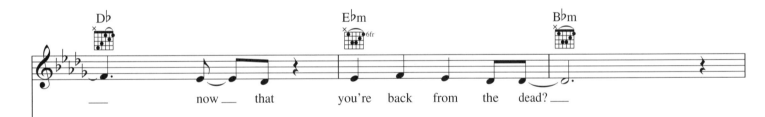

now that you're back from the dead?

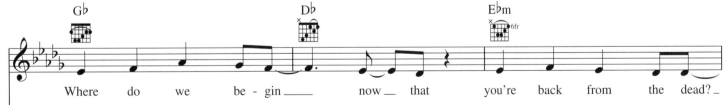

Where do we be - gin now that you're back from the dead?

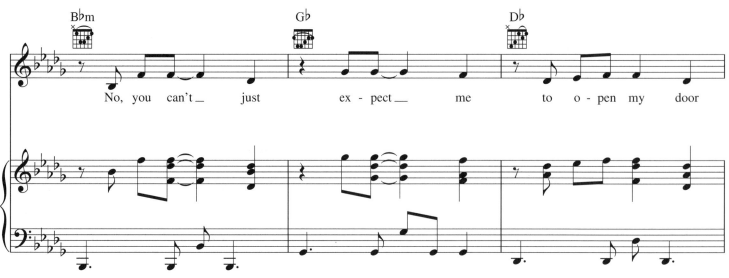

No, you can't __ just ex - pect __ me to o - pen my door

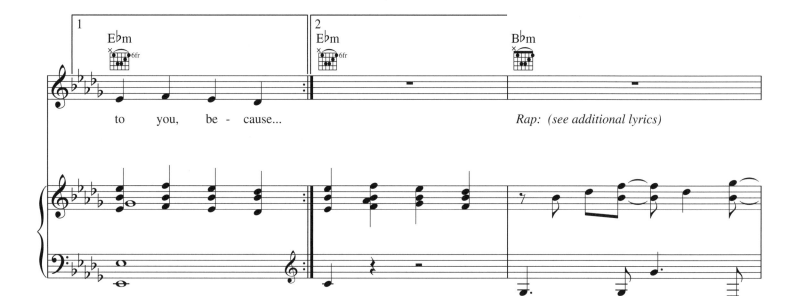

1

2

to you, be - cause... *Rap: (see additional lyrics)*

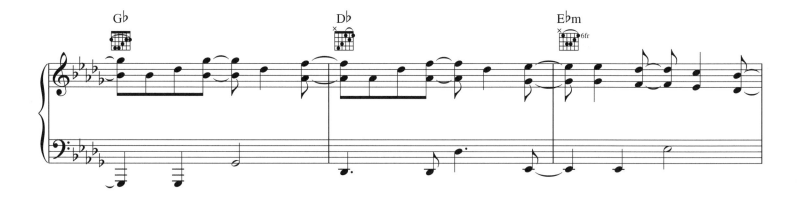

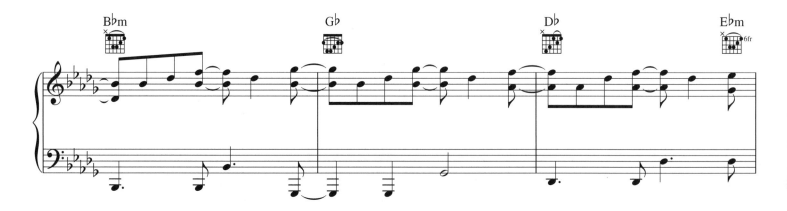

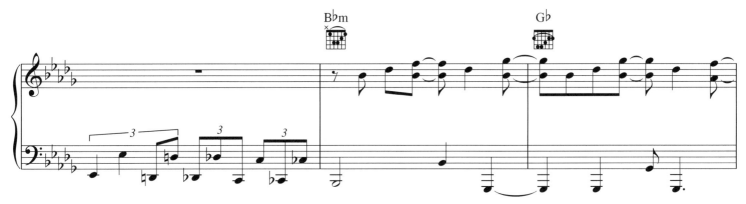

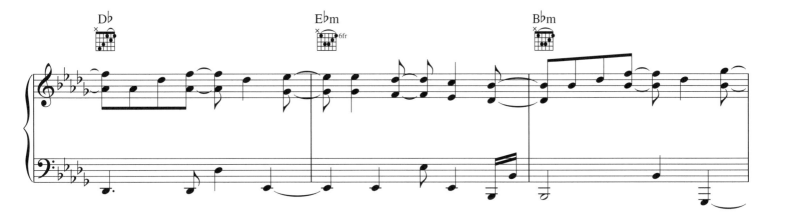

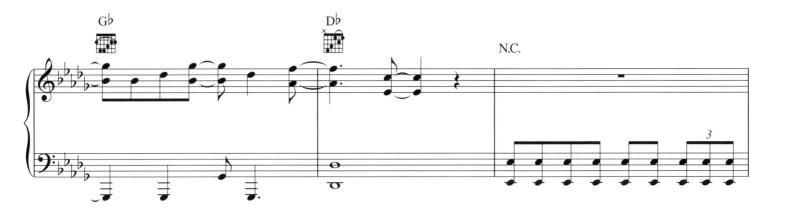

...but you gon' miss me when I'm gone. Why we

Additional Lyrics

Rap: I know, I know I can sit and talk, but I can't make you listen.
You wish that I paid attention. I thought if I paid admissions to
Wherever, go however, it would paint the perfect picture.
You said, "No matter how much you fuckin' make, it doesn't make a difference."

And I'm so, so, so sorry that we fell in love, Geronimo,
It's like, one thing leads to another. Swear we fuckin' with dominos.
But here we are. Now I'm tryin' to find an answer in this bottle, girl,
And I'm drownin' slow, drownin' slow.
Don't let the piranhas know...

Rap continues, sung (see vocal staff)

FINAL WARNING

Words and Music by SKYLAR GREY
and ALEX DA KID

WEAR ME OUT

Words and Music by SKYLAR GREY
and JONATHAN ROTEM

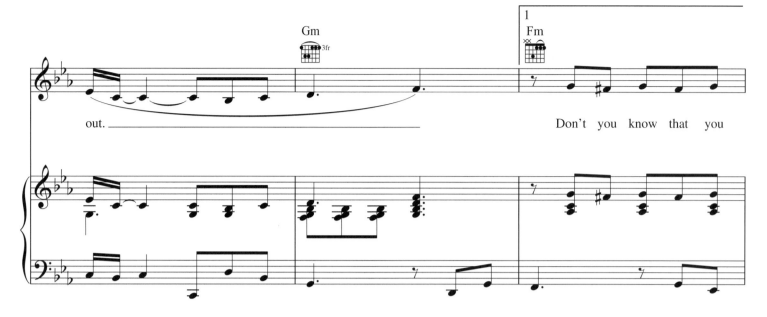

out. _____ Don't you know that you

wear   me   out. _____

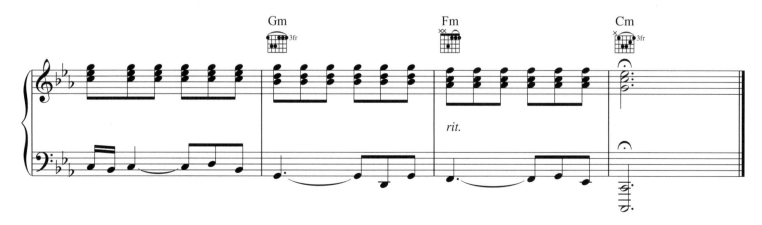

rit.

RELIGION

Words and Music by SKYLAR GREY,
JONATHAN ROTEM and IVAN CORRALIZA

It's a fucked up world that we live _____ in, _____

so let me be your re-li - gion. _____ Hey, _____ hey. _____

Repeat and Fade

Hey, _____ hey. _____

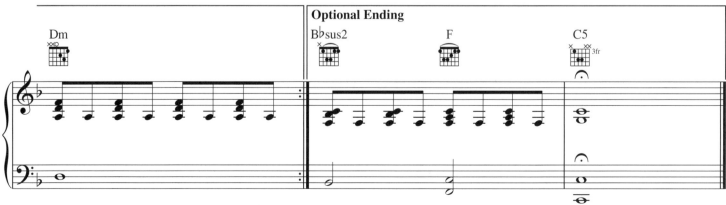

Optional Ending

C'MON LET ME RIDE

Words and Music by SKYLAR GREY,
ALEX DA KID, MIKE DEL RIO,
MARSHALL MATHERS and FREDDIE MERCURY

N.C.

Rap: (see additional lyrics)

Come on, let me ride your bi - cy - cle. It's so fan - tas - ti - cal on your bi - cy - cle.

want to ride my bi-cy-cle, you want to ride my bike.)

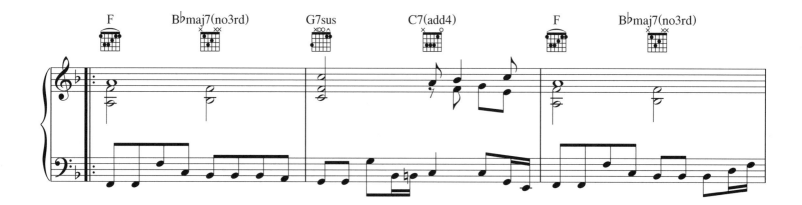

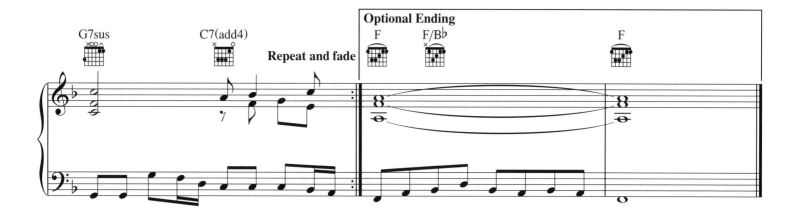

Rap: She's distracted, by my reflectors. Man I can tell this chick's attracted.
My wheels spoke to her.
My Schwinn is a chick magnet bagging up chicks like a bag of chips with
A bag of prophylactics as big as Mick Jagger lips.

Shaggin's not something I'm a pro at, But I ain't practicing shit. (Allan)
Iverson of safe sex, condoms are for practice man
I skip practice. Flip backwards while I flip this bike on its banana seat.
My fantasy's to have you land where the kickstand is.

Got this bitch gaggin', they call me the broad killa.
I'm the cousin of Godzilla 'cause I spit fire and my dick's draggin'.
Zig zaggin' up the avenue, pullin' these chicks
In my antagonist wagon, screamin'...

SUNSHINE

Words and Music by SKYLAR GREY,
ALEX DA KID and JAYSON DEZUZIO

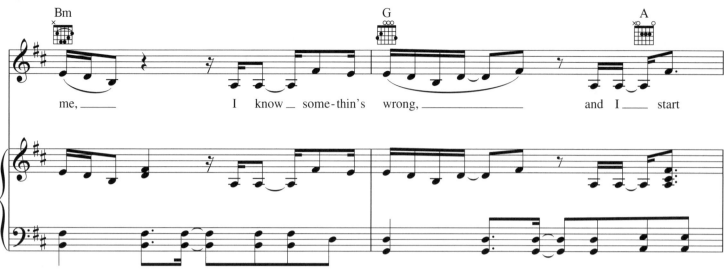

me, _____ I know ___ some-thin's wrong, _____ and I ____ start

to see _____ that this sweet ____ sun - shine ____ is the on -

- ly gold ____ I ____ need. ____

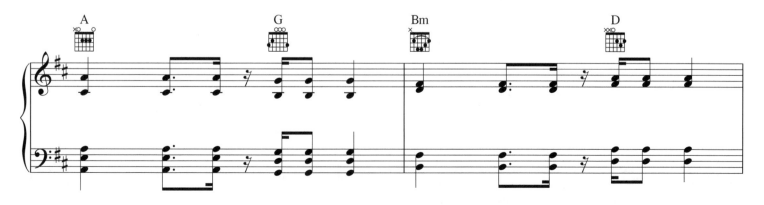

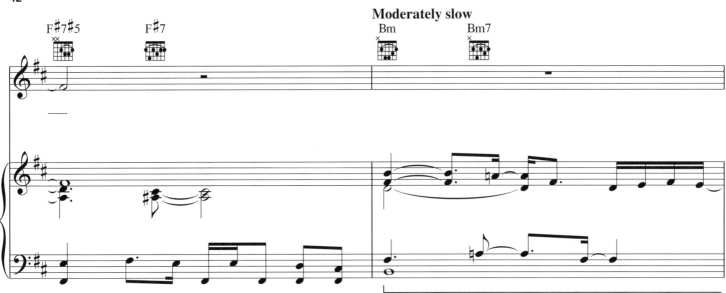

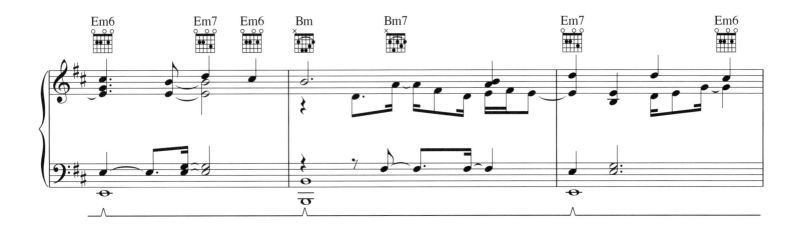

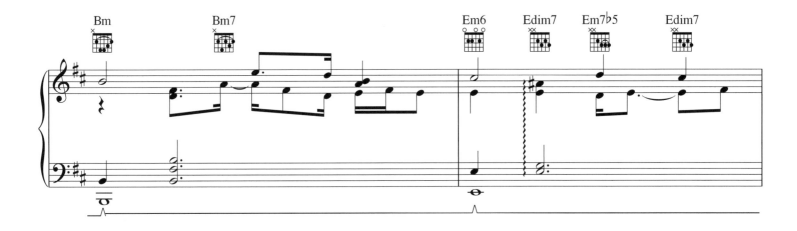

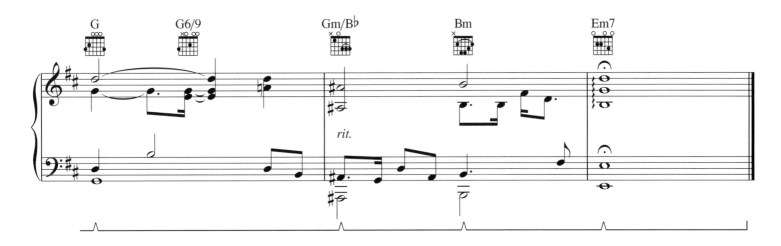

PULSE

Words and Music by SKYLAR GREY,
JAYSON DEZUZIO and JONATHAN ROTEM

Lyrics:
I heard you found a new ___ friend. ___
It's clear what you see in ___ her; ___

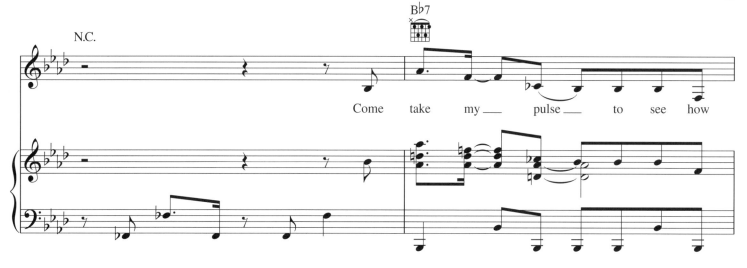

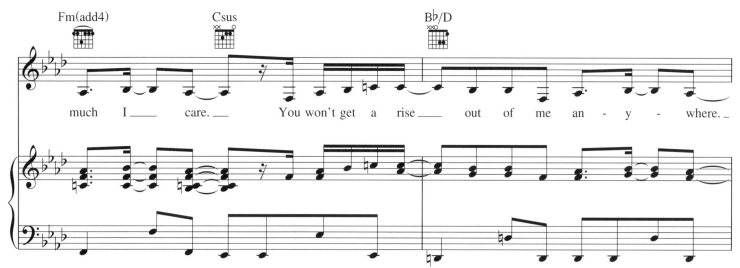

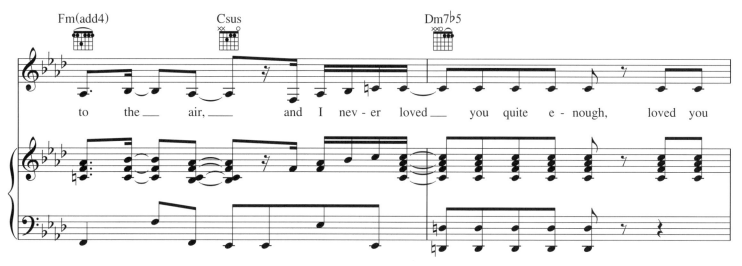

self at ____ night ____ as if you're dream - ing ___ of ___

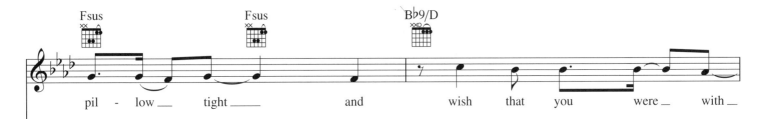

___ me. Oh, Some - times I hold my

pil - low ___ tight ____ and wish that you were _ with _

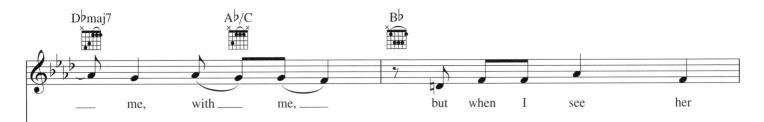

___ me, with ____ me, ____ but when I see her

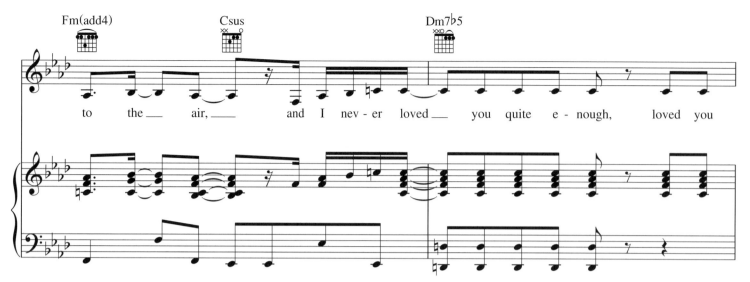

to the __ air, __ and I nev-er loved __ you quite e-nough, loved you

quite e-nough to e-ven __ care. __

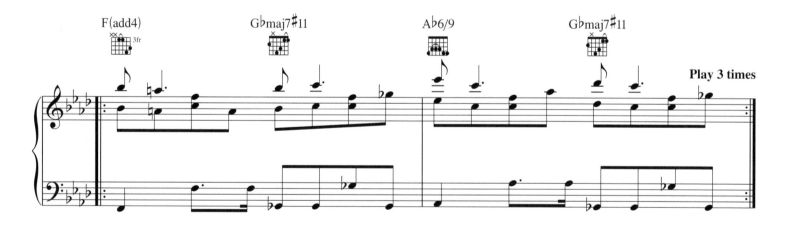

Play 3 times

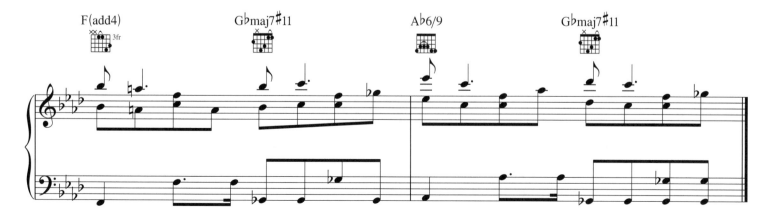

GLOW IN THE DARK

Words and Music by SKYLAR GREY,
ALEX DA KID, MIKE DEL RIO
and JAYSON DEZUZIO

glow in the dark _____ now, now, ___

___ now, now. (I've got __ it...)

(...now, now, _____ now, now.) (I've got __ it,

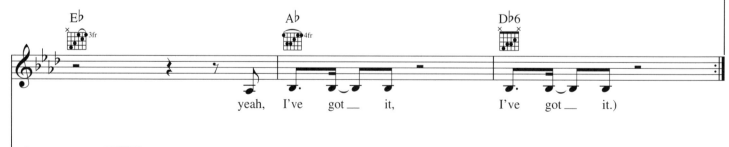

yeah, I've got __ it, I've got __ it.)

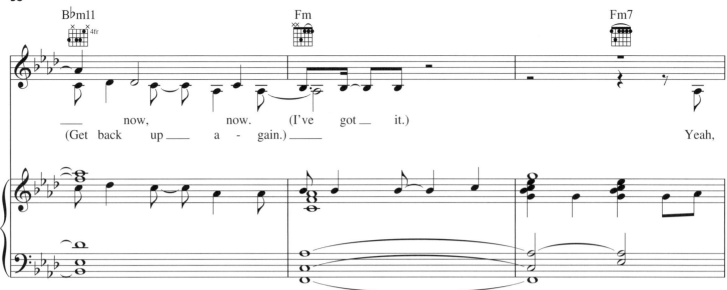

now,   now. (I've   got   it.)
(Get   back   up   a - gain.)   Yeah,

Now,   now,   now,   now.
I've   got   it,   I've   got   it.

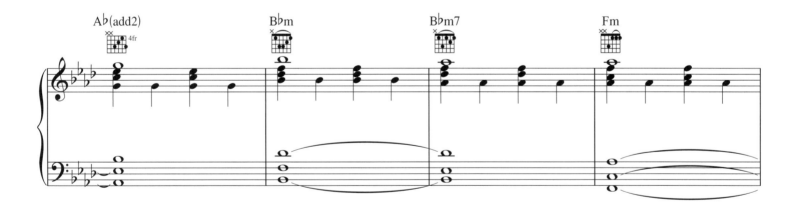

SHIT MAN!

Words and Music by SKYLAR GREY,
ALEX DA KID, JAYSON DEZUZIO
and ANGEL HAZE

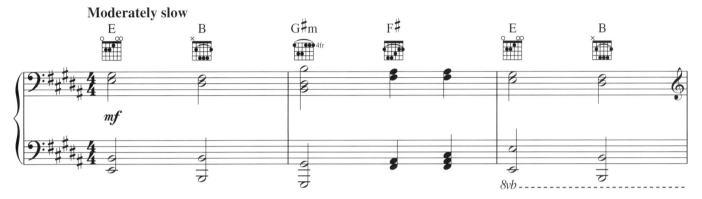

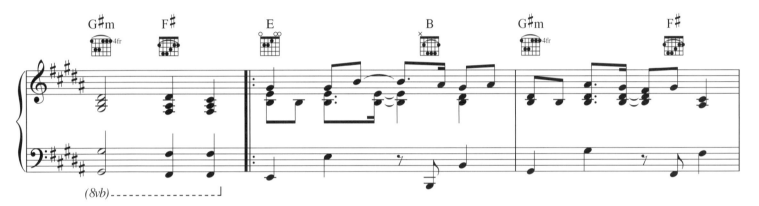

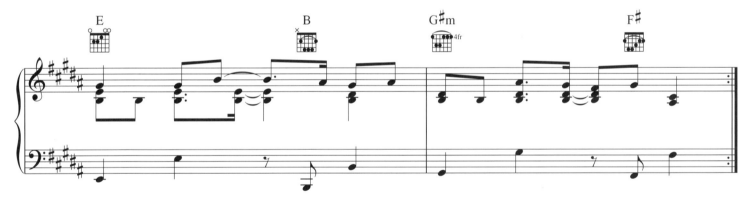

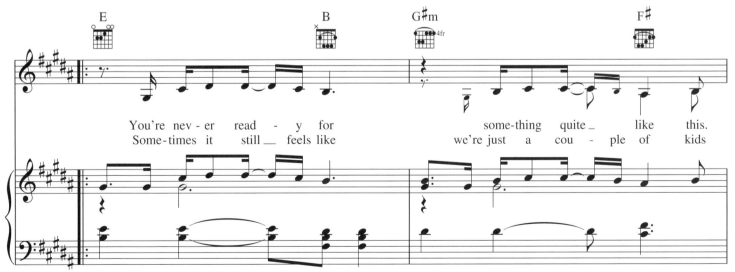

You're nev-er read-y for   some-thing quite __ like   this.
Some-times it still __ feels like   we're just a cou - ple of   kids

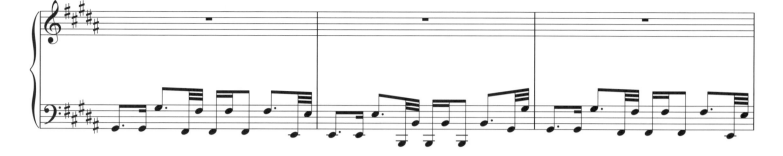

(Rap ends) How we gon - na do this

thing? How we gon - na do this shit, man? __ We don't e - ven got no

Additional Lyrics

Rap: This ain't what I expected, ain't happenin' like I thought it,
And if they say love is free, then tell me why the fuck it's costin'.
And yes, it happens often and I should cope with my losses.
And you say that you're not ready. I don't believe in abortions.

My heart, light as a feather. I know things can get better.
I know your visions's cloudy, so much inclement weather.
I know that faith is a string that's slowly coming untethered.
But we can get through anything together.

CLEAR BLUE SKY

Words and Music by SKYLAR GREY
and ALEX DA KID

Moderately fast

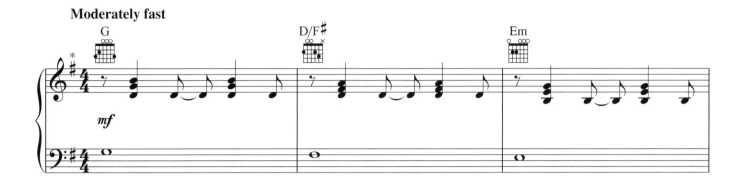

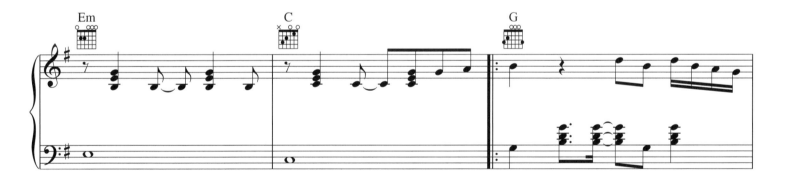

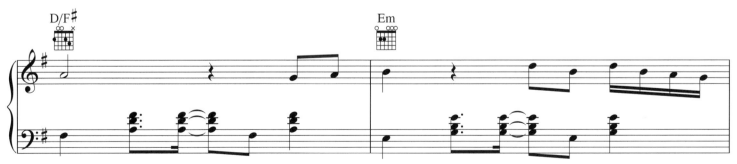

Recorded a half step lower.

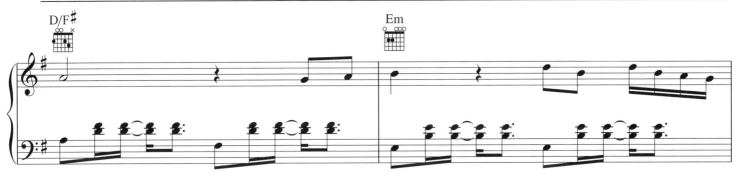

TOWER
(Don't Look Down)

Words and Music by SKYLAR GREY
and ALEX DA KID

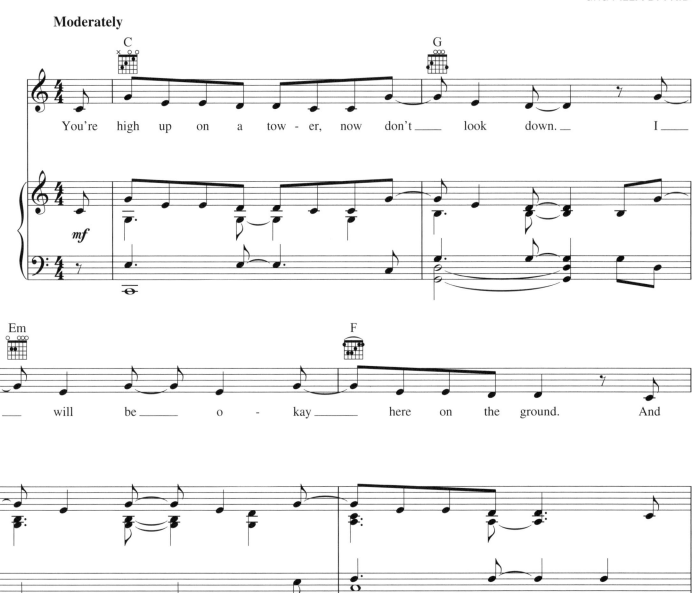

Lyrics:

You're high up on a tow-er, now don't ___ look down. ___ I ___ will be ___ o-kay ___ here on the ground. And you can al-ways call ___ to say hel-lo ___ from time to time ___

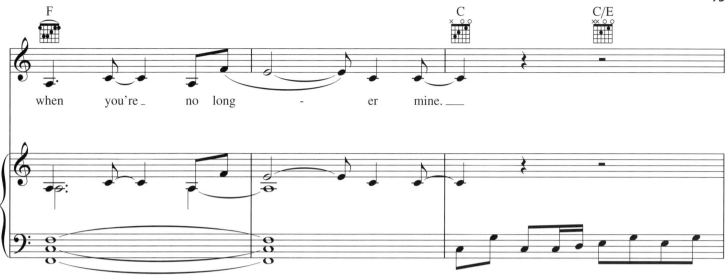

when you're __ no long - er mine. __

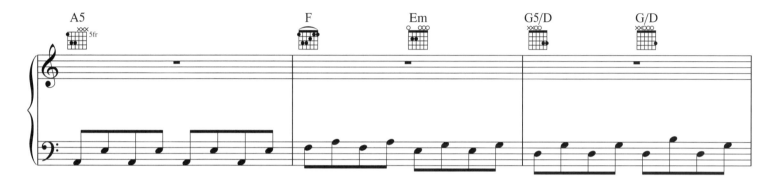

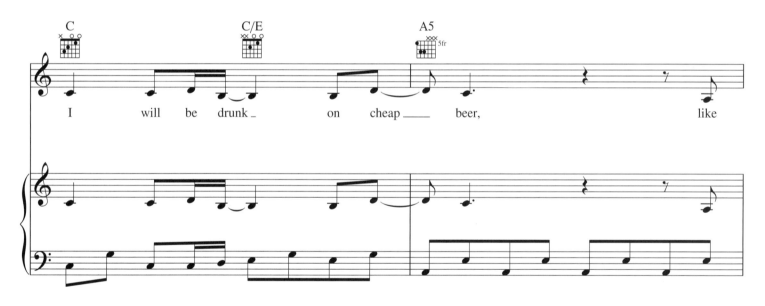

I will be drunk __ on cheap __ beer, like

ev - 'ry - one else __ a - round __ here.

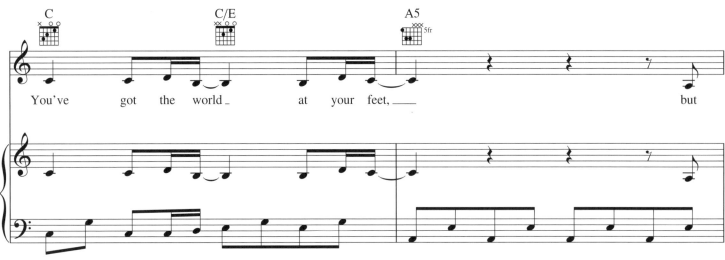

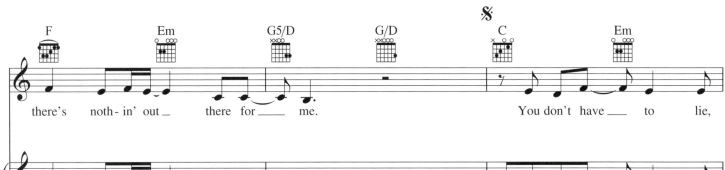

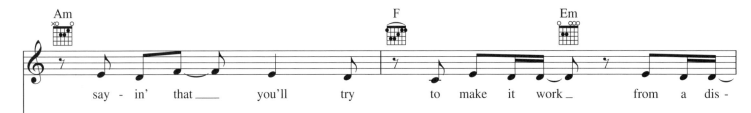

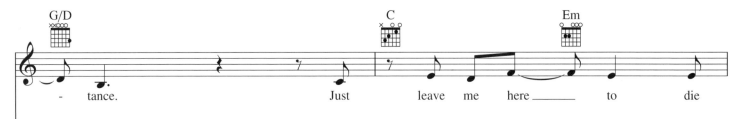

as I watch ___ you climb ___ up to the top ___ of your am - bi -

- tions. You're high up on a tow - er, now don't ___ look down. ___ I ___

___ will be ___ o - kay ___ here on the ground. And you can al - ways call ___ to say hel - lo ___

To Coda ⊕

___ from time to time ___ when you're ___ no long -

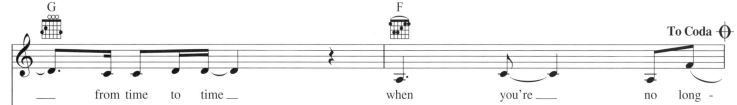

8vb -

WHITE SUBURBAN

Words and Music by
SKYLAR GREY

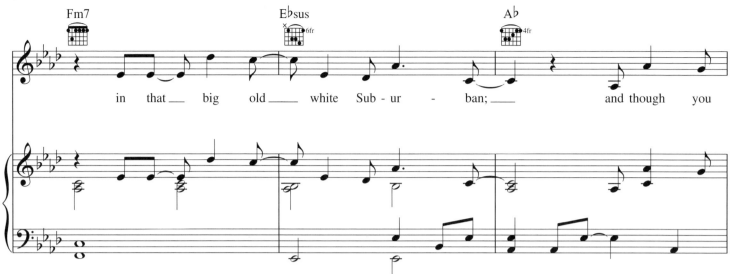

in that ___ big old ___ white Sub - ur - ban; ___ and though you

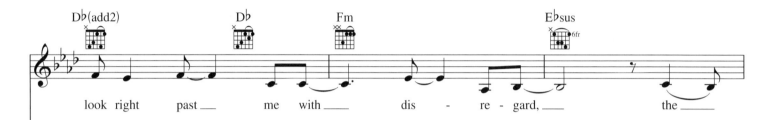

look right past ___ me with ___ dis - re - gard, ___ the ___

first won't ___ hap - pen twice.

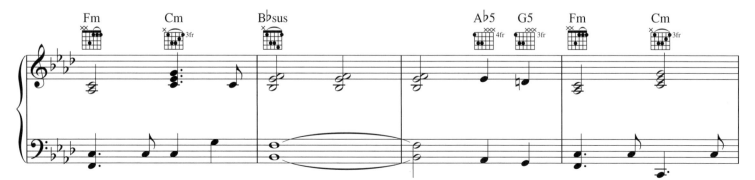

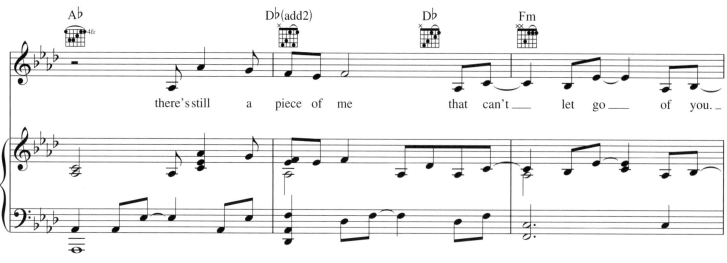

there's still a piece of me that can't ___ let go ___ of you. ___

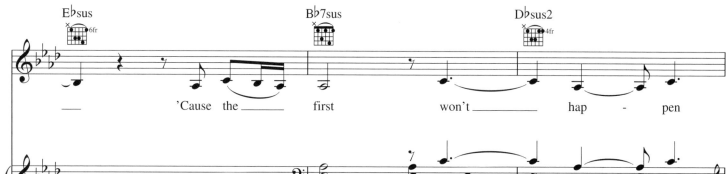

___ 'Cause the ___ first won't ___ hap - pen

rall.   *a tempo*

twice.

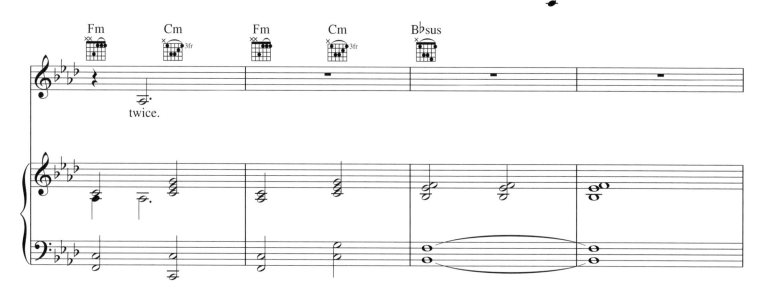

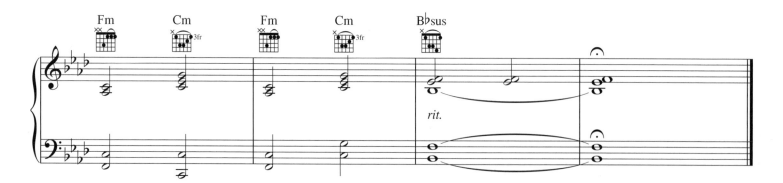

rit.